HAL•LEONARD
INSTRUMENTAL PLAY-ALONG

AUDIO ACCESS INCLUDED

PLAYBACK+
Speed • Pitch • Balance • Loop

 **VIOLA**

CHRISTMAS *Favorites*

Audio arrangements by Peter Deneff

To access audio visit:
www.halleonard.com/mylibrary

Enter Code
6086-5707-5048-6735

ISBN 978-1-4950-9641-9

T0088336

HAL•LEONARD®
7777 W. BLUEMOUND RD. P.O. BOX 13819 MILWAUKEE, WI 53213

In Australia Contact:
Hal Leonard Australia Pty. Ltd.
4 Lentara Court
Cheltenham, Victoria, 3192 Australia
Email: ausadmin@halleonard.com.au

Copyright © 2017 by HAL LEONARD LLC
International Copyright Secured   All Rights Reserved

For all works contained herein:
Unauthorized copying, arranging, adapting, recording, Internet posting, public performance,
or other distribution of the printed or recorded music in this publication is an infringement of copyright.
Infringers are liable under the law.

Visit Hal Leonard Online at
www.halleonard.com

BLUE CHRISTMAS

VIOLA

Words and Music by BILLY HAYES
and JAY JOHNSON

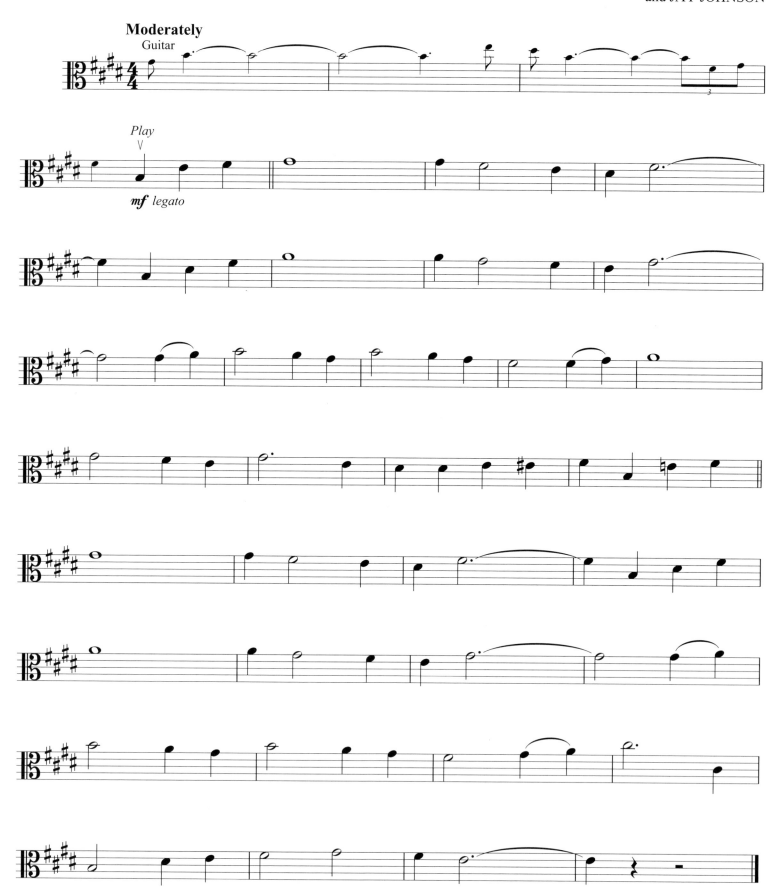

Copyright © 1948 UNIVERSAL - POLYGRAM INTERNATIONAL PUBLISHING, INC. and JUDY J. OLMSTEAD TRUST
Copyright Renewed
All Rights for JUDY J. OLMSTEAD TRUST Controlled and Administered by LICHELLE MUSIC COMPANY
All Rights Reserved   Used by Permission

THE CHRISTMAS SONG
(Chestnuts Roasting on an Open Fire)

VIOLA

Music and Lyric by MEL TORMÉ
and ROBERT WELLS

© 1946 (Renewed) EDWIN H. MORRIS & COMPANY, A Division of MPL Music Publishing, Inc. and SONY/ATV MUSIC PUBLISHING LLC
All Rights on behalf of SONY/ATV MUSIC PUBLISHING LLC Administered by SONY/ATV MUSIC PUBLISHING LLC, 424 Church Street, Suite 1200, Nashville, TN 37219
All Rights Reserved

CHRISTMAS TIME IS HERE

from A CHARLIE BROWN CHRISTMAS

VIOLA

Words by LEE MENDELSON
Music by VINCE GUARALDI

Copyright © 1966 LEE MENDELSON FILM PRODUCTIONS, INC.
Copyright Renewed
International Copyright Secured   All Rights Reserved

FELIZ NAVIDAD

VIOLA

Music and Lyrics by
JOSÉ FELICIANO

Copyright © 1970 J & H Publishing Company (ASCAP)
Copyright Renewed
All Rights Administered by Law, P.A. o/b/o J & H Publishing Company
International Copyright Secured   All Rights Reserved

HAPPY XMAS
(War Is Over)

VIOLA

Written by JOHN LENNON
and YOKO ONO

© 1971 (Renewed) LENONO MUSIC and ONO MUSIC
Administered in the United States by DOWNTOWN MUSIC PUBLISHING LLC
All Rights Reserved

HAVE YOURSELF A MERRY LITTLE CHRISTMAS

from MEET ME IN ST. LOUIS

VIOLA

Words and Music by HUGH MARTIN
and RALPH BLANE

© Copyright 1944 EMI Feist Catalog Incorporated, USA.
EMI United Partnership Limited
All Rights Reserved   International Copyright Secured
Used by permission of Music Sales Ltd.

HERE COMES SANTA CLAUS
(Right Down Santa Claus Lane)

VIOLA

Words and Music by GENE AUTRY
and OAKLEY HALDEMAN

© 1947 (Renewed) Gene Autry's Western Music Publishing Co.
All Rights Reserved   Used by Permission

(There's No Place Like)
HOME FOR THE HOLIDAYS

VIOLA

Words and Music by AL STILLMAN
and ROBERT ALLEN

© Copyright 1954 (Renewed) by Music Sales Corporation (ASCAP) and Charlie Deitcher Productions
International Copyright Secured   All Rights Reserved   Used by Permission

IT'S BEGINNING TO LOOK LIKE CHRISTMAS

VIOLA

By MEREDITH WILLSON

© 1951 PLYMOUTH MUSIC CO., INC.
© Renewed 1979 FRANK MUSIC CORP. and MEREDITH WILLSON MUSIC
All Rights Reserved

MELE KALIKIMAKA

VIOLA

Words and Music by
R. ALEX ANDERSON

Copyright © 1949 Lovely Hula Hands Music LLC
Copyright Renewed
All Rights Controlled and Administered by Lichelle Music Company
All Rights Reserved   Used by Permission

MERRY CHRISTMAS, DARLING

VIOLA

Words and Music by RICHARD CARPENTER
and FRANK POOLER

Copyright © 1970 IRVING MUSIC, INC.
Copyright Renewed
All Rights Reserved   Used by Permission

ROCKIN' AROUND THE CHRISTMAS TREE

VIOLA

Music and Lyrics by
JOHNNY MARKS

Copyright © 1958 (Renewed 1986) St. Nicholas Music Inc., 254 W. 54th Street, 12th Floor, New York, New York 10019
All Rights Reserved

RUDOLPH THE RED-NOSED REINDEER

VIOLA

Music and Lyrics by
JOHNNY MARKS

Copyright © 1949 (Renewed 1977) St. Nicholas Music Inc., 254 W. 54th Street, 12th Floor, New York, New York 10019
All Rights Reserved

SILVER AND GOLD

VIOLA

Music and Lyrics by
JOHNNY MARKS

Copyright © 1964 (Renewed 1992) St. Nicholas Music Inc., 254 W. 54th Street, 12th Floor, New York, New York 10019
All Rights Reserved

HAL•LEONARD INSTRUMENTAL PLAY-ALONG

Your favorite songs are arranged just for solo instrumentalists with this outstanding series. Each book includes a great full-accompaniment play-along audio so you can sound just like a pro! Check out **www.halleonard.com** to see all the titles available.

The Beatles

All You Need Is Love • Blackbird • Day Tripper • Eleanor Rigby • Get Back • Here, There and Everywhere • Hey Jude • I Will • Let It Be • Lucy in the Sky with Diamonds • Ob-La-Di, Ob-La-Da • Penny Lane • Something • Ticket to Ride • Yesterday.

00225330	Flute	$14.99
00225331	Clarinet	$14.99
00225332	Alto Sax	$14.99
00225333	Tenor Sax	$14.99
00225334	Trumpet	$14.99
00225335	Horn	$14.99
00225336	Trombone	$14.99
00225337	Violin	$14.99
00225338	Viola	$14.99
00225339	Cello	$14.99

Chart Hits

All About That Bass • All of Me • Happy • Radioactive • Roar • Say Something • Shake It Off • A Sky Full of Stars • Someone like You • Stay with Me • Thinking Out Loud • Uptown Funk.

00146207	Flute	$12.99
00146208	Clarinet	$12.99
00146209	Alto Sax	$12.99
00146210	Tenor Sax	$12.99
00146211	Trumpet	$12.99
00146212	Horn	$12.99
00146213	Trombone	$12.99
00146214	Violin	$12.99
00146215	Viola	$12.99
00146216	Cello	$12.99

Coldplay

Clocks • Every Teardrop Is a Waterfall • Fix You • In My Place • Lost! • Paradise • The Scientist • Speed of Sound • Trouble • Violet Hill • Viva La Vida • Yellow.

00103337	Flute	$12.99
00103338	Clarinet	$12.99
00103339	Alto Sax	$12.99
00103340	Tenor Sax	$12.99
00103341	Trumpet	$12.99
00103342	Horn	$12.99
00103343	Trombone	$12.99
00103344	Violin	$12.99
00103345	Viola	$12.99
00103346	Cello	$12.99

Disney Greats

Arabian Nights • Hawaiian Roller Coaster Ride • It's a Small World • Look Through My Eyes • Yo Ho (A Pirate's Life for Me) • and more.

00841934	Flute	$12.99
00841935	Clarinet	$12.99
00841936	Alto Sax	$12.99
00841937	Tenor Sax	$12.95
00841938	Trumpet	$12.99
00841939	Horn	$12.99
00841940	Trombone	$12.95
00841941	Violin	$12.99
00841942	Viola	$12.99
00841943	Cello	$12.99
00842078	Oboe	$12.99

Great Themes

Bella's Lullaby • Chariots of Fire • Get Smart • Hawaii Five-O Theme • I Love Lucy • The Odd Couple • Spanish Flea • and more.

00842468	Flute	$12.99
00842469	Clarinet	$12.99
00842470	Alto Sax	$12.99
00842471	Tenor Sax	$12.99
00842472	Trumpet	$12.99
00842473	Horn	$12.99
00842474	Trombone	$12.99
00842475	Violin	$12.99
00842476	Viola	$12.99
00842477	Cello	$12.99

Popular Hits

Breakeven • Fireflies • Halo • Hey, Soul Sister • I Gotta Feeling • I'm Yours • Need You Now • Poker Face • Viva La Vida • You Belong with Me • and more.

00842511	Flute	$12.99
00842512	Clarinet	$12.99
00842513	Alto Sax	$12.99
00842514	Tenor Sax	$12.99
00842515	Trumpet	$12.99
00842516	Horn	$12.99
00842517	Trombone	$12.99
00842518	Violin	$12.99
00842519	Viola	$12.99
00842520	Cello	$12.99

Songs from Frozen, Tangled and Enchanted

Do You Want to Build a Snowman? • For the First Time in Forever • Happy Working Song • I See the Light • In Summer • Let It Go • Mother Knows Best • That's How You Know • True Love's First Kiss • When Will My Life Begin • and more.

00126921	Flute	$14.99
00126922	Clarinet	$14.99
00126923	Alto Sax	$14.99
00126924	Tenor Sax	$14.99
00126925	Trumpet	$14.99
00126926	Horn	$14.99
00126927	Trombone	$14.99
00126928	Violin	$14.99
00126929	Viola	$14.99
00126930	Cello	$14.99

Top Hits

Adventure of a Lifetime • Budapest • Die a Happy Man • Ex's & Oh's • Fight Song • Hello • Let It Go • Love Yourself • One Call Away • Pillowtalk • Stitches • Writing's on the Wall.

00171073	Flute	$12.99
00171074	Clarinet	$12.99
00171075	Alto Sax	$12.99
00171106	Tenor Sax	$12.99
00171107	Trumpet	$12.99
00171108	Horn	$12.99
00171109	Trombone	$12.99
00171110	Violin	$12.99
00171111	Viola	$12.99
00171112	Cello	$12.99

Wicked

As Long As You're Mine • Dancing Through Life • Defying Gravity • For Good • I'm Not That Girl • Popular • The Wizard and I • and more.

00842236	Flute	$12.99
00842237	Clarinet	$12.99
00842238	Alto Saxophone	$11.95
00842239	Tenor Saxophone	$11.95
00842240	Trumpet	$11.95
00842241	Horn	$11.95
00842242	Trombone	$12.99
00842243	Violin	$11.99
00842244	Viola	$12.99
00842245	Cello	$12.99

Prices, contents, and availability subject to change without notice.
Disney characters and artwork © Disney Enterprises, Inc.

HAL•LEONARD®

0617